Prince Dighavu

OpenDust™, Inc.
www.opendustpublish.com

Prince Dighavu

Published by OpenDust, Inc.
P.O. Box 19036, Oakland, California 94619 USA
www.opendustpublish.com
service@opendustpublish.com

Editor:	Brian Conroy
Illustrator:	Charlene Wong
Layout :	Ya-Yun Pan / Elaine Ginn
Logo:	Chi-Chang Weng
Storyteller:	Brian Conroy

Library of Congress Control Number: 2007941821

ISBN 978-1-60236-003-7

First Edition
1 2 3 4 5 6 7 8 9 08

Printed by Shyh Hyah International Co., Ltd., Taiwan, R.O.C.

Prince Dighavu

Retold by Brian Conroy
with audio CD

Illustrated by Charlene Wong

OpenDust, Inc.
Oakland, California
opendustpublish.com

OpenDust, Inc.

*Dust (Ignorance) broken,
Sutras (Wisdom) revealed,
To benefit all beings.*

Acknowledgements

The story of *Prince Dighavu* is adapted from
the Buddhist Canon. We appreciate the teachings
from all the Awakened Sages.

Special thanks to Dharma Master Heng Lung for
her kind and patient guidance in layout and publishing.
Another special thanks to Priscilla Wong for
introducing the teachings of the Awakened
Sages of the past, present, and those to come,
into the life of artist Charlene Wong.
To all of them we give our thanks.

May all beings be happy and peaceful.

May this story be inspiring and reflect:

Caring

Repaying kindness

Sincerity

Patience

Kindness

Bravery

Friendship

Forgiveness

Generosity

Gratefulness

कोशल

काशी

In olden times,
the kingdoms of Kāśī and Kośala
lay side by side.

Brahmadatta,
the king of Kāśī,
was a powerful
ruler with a strong
army and well
filled treasuries.

King Dighiti, who ruled
the kingdom of Kośala,
had a smaller army
and meager treasuries.

5

Brahmadatta,
seeing how easy it would be
to overpower
the smaller kingdom,
decided to conquer Kośala.

When King Dighiti saw
that Brahmadatta's army
was approaching,
he knew he did not
stand a chance.

8

To avoid bloodshed,
he surrendered his army.

9

Because the king and
the queen so loved their young
son, Prince Dighavu, and wanted
to spare him from being killed at
the hands of Brahmadatta, they
dressed him in common clothes
and sent him to live in the
countryside.

12

The last words King Dighiti
spoke to his son were these:

"Do not look long!
Do not look short!
Hatred cannot be stopped by hatred.
Hatred can only be stopped by love."

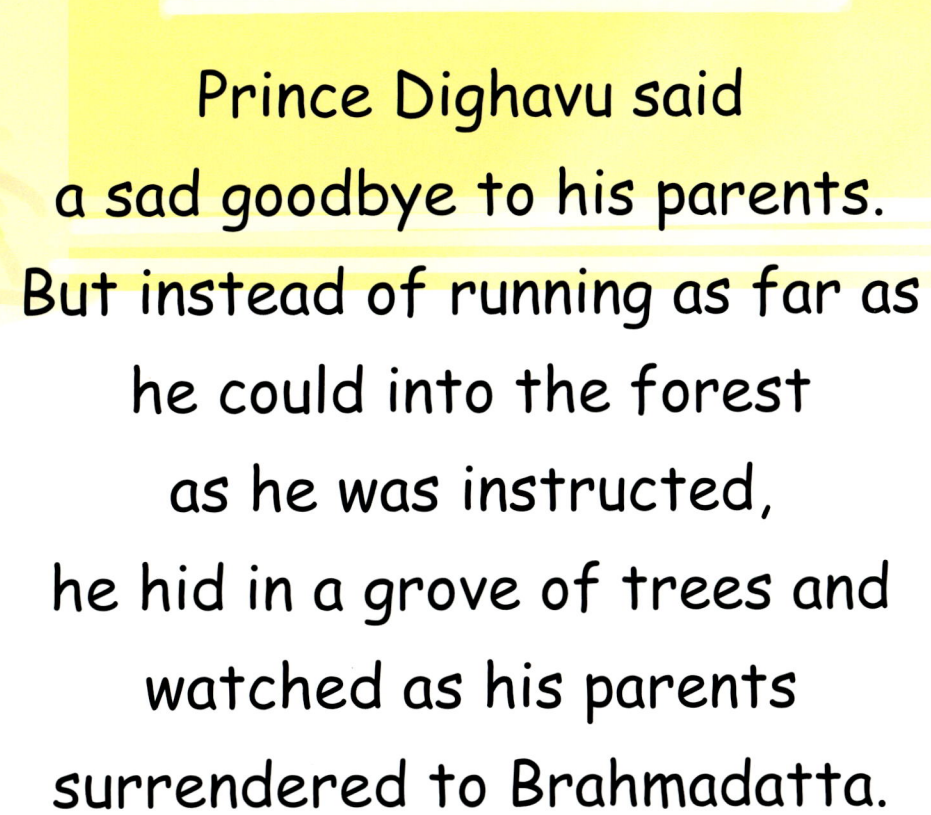

Prince Dighavu said
a sad goodbye to his parents.
But instead of running as far as
he could into the forest
as he was instructed,
he hid in a grove of trees and
watched as his parents
surrendered to Brahmadatta.

Their arms were tied
behind their backs,
their heads were shaved,
and to the loud beating of a drum
they were paraded
through the streets
to their execution.

Helplessly, the young prince
watched as Brahmadatta killed
both of his parents. As tears
streamed down his face, a bitter
fire of hatred was sparked in his soul
and he vowed that
if it took him his entire life,
he would gain revenge
against King Brahmadatta.

He wandered in the forest,
lost, thinking of nothing else
but how he would exact his revenge.

One morning he heard the sound
of a musician who sang and
played music with such charm
that all living things stopped
to listen when he played.

23

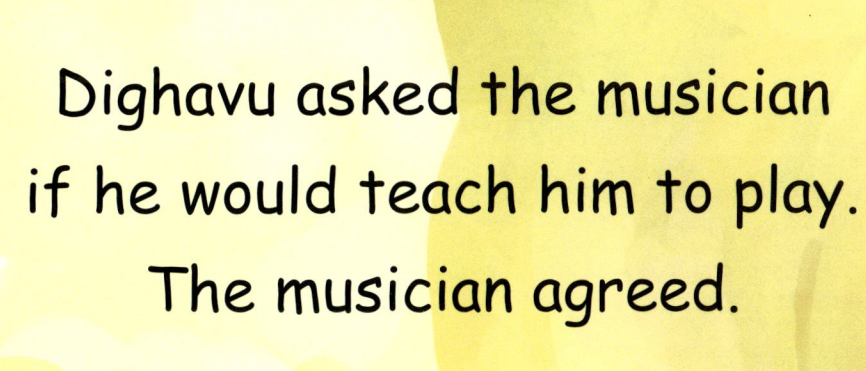

Dighavu asked the musician
if he would teach him to play.
The musician agreed.

Dighavu lived with the musician
and for years he practiced his art.

So well did the musician teach
Dighavu that when the young
prince played his music
the air stood still,
wild animals were tamed
and babies stopped crying.

Years passed until one day Brahmadatta happened to be traveling through that part of the forest and chanced to hear Dighavu's music.

He found it so enchanting that
he stopped and ask Dighavu
if he would travel with him
on his journeys and play music
to soothe his spirit.

Prince Dighavu saw that the king
had no idea he was the son
of the King of Kośala,
so he quickly agreed.

From that day forward Prince Dighavu
and King Brahmadatta traveled together.
The prince played his music so well
and proved to be such a good servant
that he rose to a high position
in the court of the king.
In time, he became the king's
most trusted confidant.

One day, Dighavu and
Brahmadatta went out hunting.

Late in the day,
the king grew tired
and told Dighavu
that he would
like to rest.

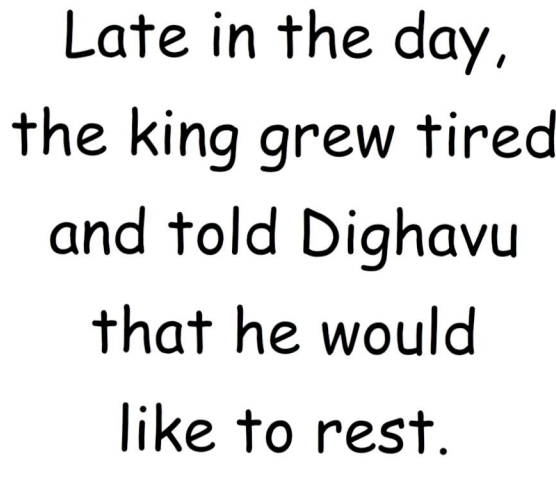

Dighavu spread a blanket
on the ground.

Brahmadatta lay down, and placed
his head on Dighavu's lap.

And in time
fell fast asleep.

Dighavu knew that
his patience had paid off.
He drew his sword,
raised it up over his head,
and brought it down to cut
the throat of Brahmadatta.

But as he did
he heard the words of his father
echo in the stillness of the forest air.

"Do not look long!
Do not look short!

Hatred cannot be
stopped by hatred.

Hatred can only be
stopped by love."

Though his hatred for
Brahmadatta was strong,
his love for his parents was stronger,
so he returned the sword
to its sheath.

But then his hatred overpowered him,
and once again he drew the sword.
Once again he heard the words
of his father echo in the air,
and he returned the sword
to its sheath.

A third time
he drew his sword;

a third time he
heard his father's words;

a third time he
returned the sword
to its sheath.

Suddenly the king awakened, startled,
frightened as if from a nightmare.
"What is the matter, your majesty?"

"I dreamed,"
said the king,

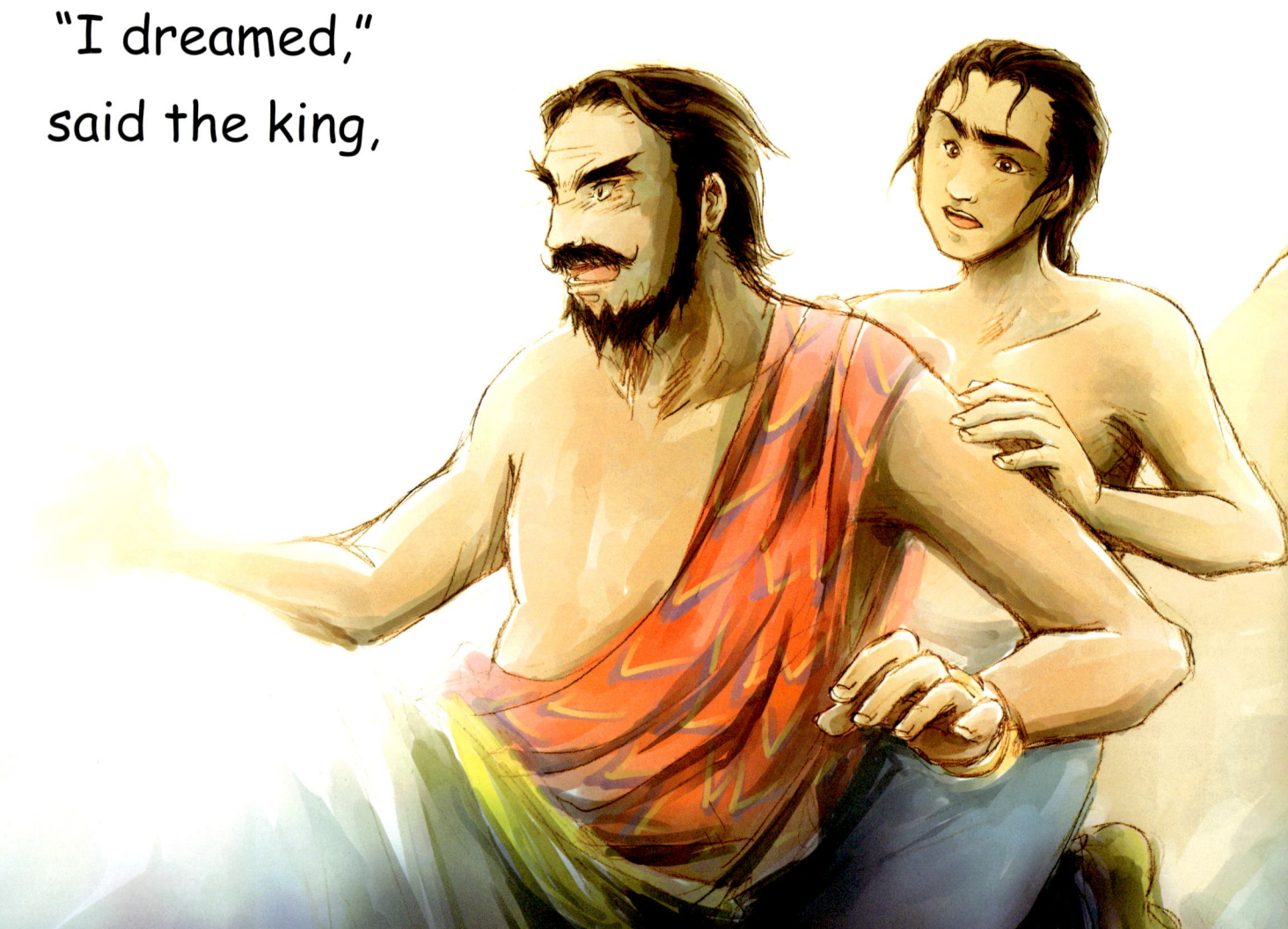

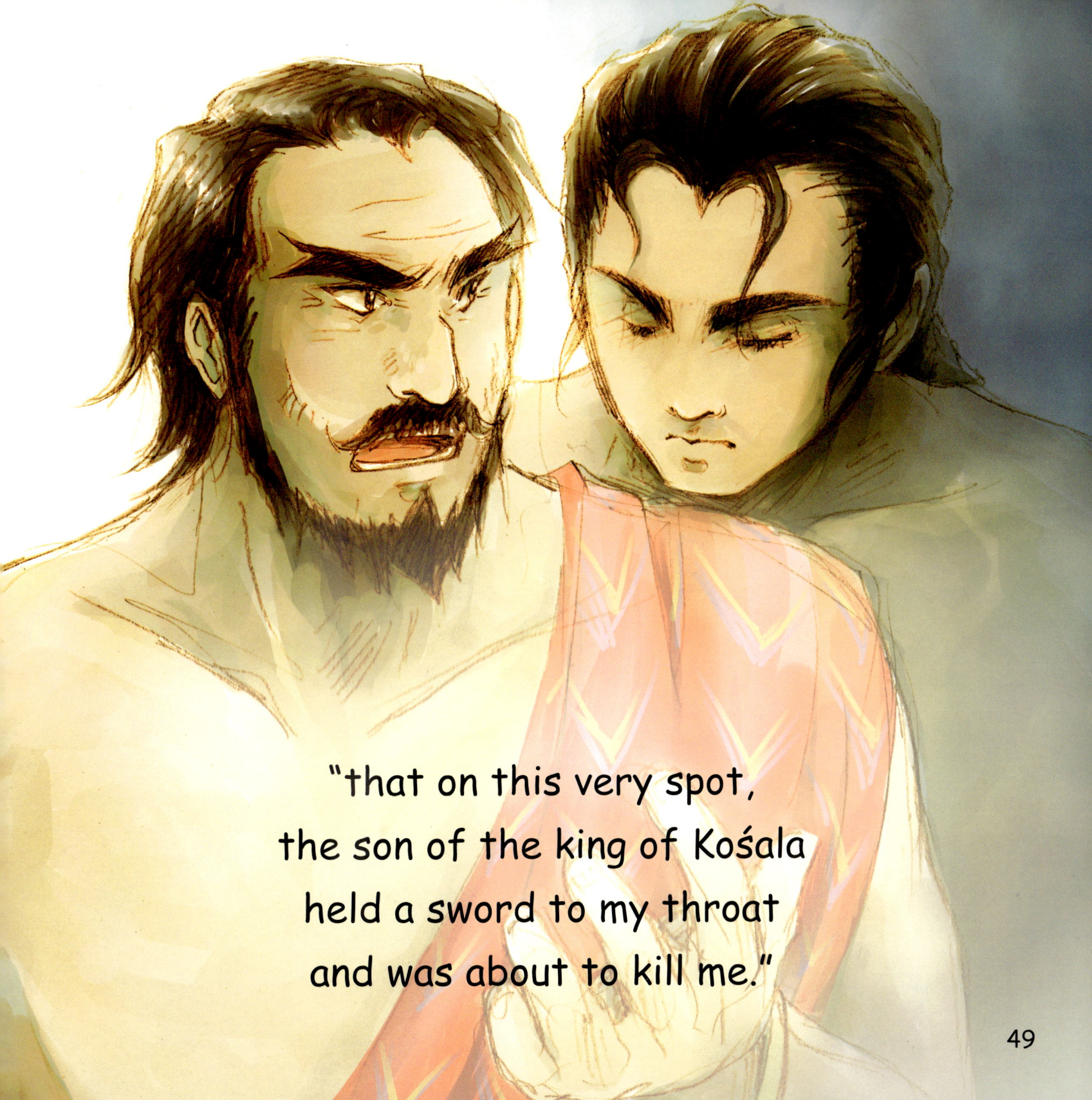

"that on this very spot,
the son of the king of Kośala
held a sword to my throat
and was about to kill me."

49

Dighavu grabbed the hair of
Brahmadatta with his left hand
and drew the sword
with his right hand and said,
"I am the son of the king of Kośala.
You have taken our kingdom,
robbed our treasuries, and made
our soldiers prisoners!
Now it is time for me
to satisfy my hatred!"

The king placed his palms together
and begged for mercy,
but Dighavu heard him not.
He drew his sword,
raised it over head,
and brought it down
to cut the throat
of Brahmadatta.

But when he did
he heard the words
of his father,
so loudly this time
he could hear nothing else.

"Do not look long!
Do not look short!

Hatred cannot be
stopped by hatred.

Hatred can only be
stopped by love."

55

He began to understand.
He relaxed his grip on
the sword and said,

"What good would it do
if I kill you?

"If I kill you, your son will kill me,
and my son will kill him and on
and on until the end of time.

"But we two can put an end to the hatred between our kingdoms."

"Yes,"
said
the king,

58

"You grant me my life
and I will grant you your life."

The prince buried his sword
in its sheath and
buried his hatred
in his heart.

When he did, he finally understood
the words of his father.
He explained them to the king.

61

"When my father said,
'Do not look long,' he meant:
Do not hold onto hatred long.

"When he said,
'Do not look short,'
he meant:
Do not be short
on forgiveness.

"For hatred cannot be stopped
by more hatred.
Hatred can only be stopped
by love."

66

The prince and
the king embraced
and swore an oath
never to harm
each other.

And to this day
the kingdoms of Kāśī and Kośala
are living in peace.